WEALTH IS A MINDSET

The power of a wealthy mindset in living a prosperous life.

Samantha Jones

TABLE OF CONTENT

CHAPTER 1

INTRODUCTION

Although it's far more common to associate wealth with the accumulation of cash and things, wealth unquestionably includes more than simply material possessions.
Wealth is a whole way of life that consists of relationships, health, and enjoyment. This book addresses the belief in wealth as a mindset and offers the foundation for knowing how to gain it.

The first step to reaching wealth is understanding that it's far more than simply cash. Each aspect of who we are as people is infused with the attitude that we must be prosperous. Residing abundantly involves having masses of everything we need and being happy with what we currently have. This isn't always to say that cash is irrelevant; instead, it shouldn't be the whole cognizance of our lifestyles. While we embody the mindset of gathering wealth, we can be triumphant and feel greater fulfillment in each aspect of our lives.

If we need to be affluent, we need to adopt the right mindset. This indicates that we want to trade how we think about achievement for wealth. Many people believe that the best individuals who can be successful are those who are lucky or have been born into wealth. But this is inaccurate. Anyone can become wealthy; however, it takes a certain mindset to accomplish so. Step one in developing the right mindset is figuring out that obtaining wealth is more of an adventure than a destination.

Staying power, perseverance, and labor are required in this by-no-means-finishing process of increase and development. It's miles more critical to set affordable dreams and make regular progress toward them than to search for instant gratification. To do that, we ought to shift our recognition from short-term advantage to long-term fulfillment.

An important element of the wealth mindset is gratitude. It's essential to be pleased with what we do have rather than specializing in what we don't. Via being grateful, we can also make use of the money we have already got and appeal to greater. Gratitude makes us more receptive to new possibilities and experiences, which could help us obtain more economic fulfillment. Being thankful is vital, but so is maintaining a positive mindset.

Many people have bad views about money, including the idea that fulfillment begets selfishness and greed or that it is the basis of all evil. These concepts may want to preserve us from achieving monetary success.

By adopting a high-quality outlook on money and success, we may additionally triumph over these restricting thoughts and attract more prosperity into our lives.

Last but not least, developing a mindset of prosperity requires a dedication to lifelong learning and improvement. We need to be keen to fix our mistakes and preserve improvement.

To obtain our dreams, this includes making monetary investments in education, searching out mentors and coaches, and taking calculated risks. By adopting a boom mentality, we can overcome barriers and achieve greater success in all spheres of our lives.

In conclusion, having wealth means having a complete way of life that places relationships, health, and pleasure above monetary balance. To turn out to be affluent, we need to broaden the proper attitude, which incorporates transferring our recognition from brief-term gains to long-term achievement, being grateful, having a high-quality mindset towards cash and achievement, and being committed to lifelong learning and private development. With the aid of adopting a wealth mindset, we can enjoy extra success and achievement in all aspects of our lives.

CHAPTER 2

CHANGING YOUR MINDSET

It's crucial to first assess one's thinking if one wants to become wealthy. This chapter examines the many attitudes that people might adopt and offers doable advice on altering one's mindset to better acquire prosperity.

A scarcity mindset and a growth mindset are the two primary categories of mindsets. A scarcity mindset is characterized by the conviction that our skills and intelligence are unchangeable and fixed. This kind of thinking can be constrictive and prevent us from reaching our greatest potential.

This way of thinking is defined by the conviction that there are not enough resources and that they are scarce.

Those who have a scarcity mindset frequently concentrate on what they don't have or what they are unable to do rather than what they do have and how they may use it. This might make it challenging to succeed financially and cause feelings of worry and anxiety.
It takes conscious effort to shift from a mindset of scarcity to one of abundance. Recognizing and replacing your negative thought patterns is one of the first stages.

Also, using encouraging words can help. This may entail reorienting your perspective and emphasizing issues rather than solutions. Using encouraging words to boost confidence and overcome self-doubt is another option.

Contrarily, a growth mindset, also known as an abundance mindset, is characterized by the conviction that our skills and intelligence can be improved through perseverance and hard work. To get wealthy, one must adopt this mindset.

Those who have an abundance attitude think there is more than enough for everyone. They put more emphasis on their strengths than their flaws, and they perceive opportunities where others see hurdles. An increase in self-assurance and optimism as well as increased financial success might result from this approach.

Challenges should be welcomed and seen as chances for growth to cultivate a growth mindset. We should seek out challenges as a chance to learn new abilities and get beyond hurdles rather than avoid them. Additionally, we ought to be open to learning from our errors and view failure as a springboard for progress. This calls for a change in mindset from a fear of failing to a readiness to take chances.

The ability to think positively is a crucial component in developing a growth mindset. Focusing on the good aspects of a situation rather than focusing on the bad is known as positive thinking.
Positive thinking helps us attract more optimism into our lives and conquer challenges more quickly. This calls for a change in our way of thinking, away from a focus on constraints and toward a focus on possibilities.

Another effective strategy for shifting your perspective is visualization. You can visualize your desired outcome by picturing yourself as prosperous. This can assist you in maintaining motivation and focus on your objectives, as well as make it simpler for you to get past roadblocks.

It's crucial to surround yourself with supportive people. In addition to looking for mentors and role models who have achieved financial success, this might also involve reading books and listening to podcasts about personal finance and wealth creation. You can benefit from their experiences and obtain insightful knowledge about how to become wealthy by surrounding yourself with people who have an abundant mindset.

It's critical to act in the direction of your goals in addition to altering your mentality. Setting financial objectives and developing a strategy to achieve them might be part of this. It could also entail taking chances and putting yourself in uncomfortable situations to explore opportunities for development and achievement.

The development of thankfulness and appreciation for what you currently have is crucial. You can cultivate a sense of abundance and draw more fulfilling experiences into your life by concentrating on the good things in your life. This might make it simpler for you to reach financial achievement by assisting you in maintaining your motivation and concentrating on your goals.

In conclusion, a critical element to attaining riches is altering your thinking. By recognizing and altering unproductive thought habits, picturing accomplishment, and surrounding
You can attain financial success by surrounding yourself with supportive people, making progress toward your goals, and practicing thankfulness and appreciation.

CHAPTER 3

DEFINING WEALTH

Having discussed how crucial it is to alter one's thinking to become wealthy, it is critical to examine what money is. Depending on how a person views it, wealth may be described in a variety of ways. For some, being wealthy may simply refer to possessing a lot of money or material goods. Others might view it as encompassing a larger definition of abundance, such as contentment, happiness, and deep connections.

It's crucial to remember that a person's perspective on money might affect their thinking and method of acquiring it. A person may acquire a scarcity mindset and concentrate only on acquiring riches at all costs if they think that wealth is simply about having money and material stuff.

Those who see money as encompassing a larger definition of abundance, on the other hand, could be more inclined to adopt an abundance mindset and concentrate on acquiring riches in a way that is consistent with their values and beliefs.

Many different things can help someone become wealthy. A person's capacity for earning money and accumulating wealth can be influenced by their education, talents, and experience, which are all significant aspects.

People can acquire the information and skills needed to pursue better-paying jobs and career prospects through education.

Also, it can serve as a base for entrepreneurship and business ownership. Technical and soft skills, such as leadership and communication, can have an impact on a person's earning potential and career options. People with valuable skills are frequently in high demand and can charge higher incomes or fees.

Another crucial element in acquiring riches is experience. Years of experience in a certain business or field may increase a person's likelihood of developing significant networks and knowledge that open up new chances and provide financial rewards. Having a network of encouraging relationships is another crucial aspect of being wealthy.

Those who can offer guidance, encouragement, and chances for development and advancement include mentors, coworkers, friends, and family members. The ability to collaborate and communicate effectively are two talents that people can gain by cultivating great relationships and which can be beneficial in both personal and professional settings.

Furthermore crucial is having a firm grasp of personal finance and adopting wise financial practices. This includes planning a budget, putting money down for the future, and staying out of debt. An individual can lay a solid basis for long-term wealth-building by taking charge of their finances.

It's crucial to keep in mind that while these elements might undoubtedly contribute to wealth, they are not the only ones at work. Another set of elements, such as good fortune, timing, and resource availability, can also affect a person's capacity for wealth accumulation.

In the end, having money means having the right mindset, abilities, and opportunities. It's critical to have a comprehensive approach to wealth creation, emphasizing not only financial success but also personal fulfillment and happiness.

In conclusion, the process of defining wealth is intricate and multifaceted, and it is influenced by each person's thoughts and ideas. Wealth can be influenced by several factors, including education, talents, and experience, but these are not the only ones at work.

In the end, acquiring wealth necessitates a holistic strategy that integrates monetary success, personal satisfaction, and a sense of abundance and thankfulness. People can put themselves in a position for increased prosperity by obtaining relevant skills and experiences and adopting an abundance mindset.

CHAPTER 4

PLANNING YOUR WEALTH

For one to achieve independence and financial stability, a sound wealth plan must be created. Setting clear goals and ensuring they are in line with your values is crucial to coming up with a strategy that works for you. This can help you identify your financial goals and the steps necessary to achieve them.

To start a wealth strategy, one of the first tasks is to decide what your financial objectives are. Your goals must be specific, measurable, time-bound, and relevant. This means that you should establish goals that are specific, measurable, and reasonable, as well as assign yourself a deadline to meet those goals.

You could, for instance, decide to save a certain amount of money over a certain length of time or to pay off a certain obligation.

Create a budget that will help you reach your goals after you've decided what they are. A budget is an essential tool that can assist you in keeping track of your earnings and outgoing costs, identifying areas where you can cut costs, and ensuring that you are allocating enough money to achieve your goals.

Make sure to include both fixed and variable costs in your budget by considering all of your spendings. You will have a clear grasp of your financial condition as a result, and you will be able to make decisions regarding your spending with confidence.

Another crucial element of developing a successful financial plan is investing in yourself. This entails spending money on your training, abilities, and personal development. Your marketability rises as a result of your ongoing learning and improvement, which may open up more financial and professional options for you.

Also, investing in yourself can assist you in acquiring new abilities that may result in new company initiatives or additional sources of revenue.
Gaining wealth requires taking measured risks, which is another crucial step. This entails being prepared to accept calculated risks, such as making stock market investments or starting a new company.

It's crucial to realize that taking chances shouldn't be done carelessly. Instead, it should be supported by thorough investigation and analysis and built upon a clear comprehension of the benefits and hazards.

Ultimately, developing a wealth plan is a continuous process. To keep it current and functional, it needs to be continually assessed and modified. This entails routinely assessing your objectives, spending plan, and investing tactics to make sure they are still consistent with your values and priorities as an individual. It's also critical to keep up with market movements and other developments that can affect your financial condition.

In conclusion, putting together a successful wealth plan includes having specific objectives, making a budget, investing in oneself, taking cautious risks, and continuing to evaluate and change the plan.

These stages might help you develop a strategy that supports your principles and leads to financial security and independence. Do not forget that developing a wealth plan is more of a journey than a goal. The rewards could be substantial, but it requires time, work, and commitment.

CHAPTER 5

FOUNDATIONS OF CREATING WEALTH

1.1. A CONTINUOUS LEARNING

Learning should always be a constant process. It is crucial for our professional and financial success in addition to being helpful for our personal growth and development.

The importance of education cannot be stressed in the world we live in today, especially in terms of generating money. Let's look at how learning can make us rich as an example of this.
Learning mostly aids in the development of new abilities and information. The abilities

and knowledge we acquire via learning are crucial for building wealth, whether we are learning a new programming language, a new marketing approach, or a new way to handle our finances.

For instance, a businessperson who takes the time to research a new market trend may utilize that information to develop a brand-new good or service that caters to the demands of that market. More sales and revenue might follow, which would generate wealth.

Also, learning enables us to remain competitive and relevant in the employment market. Many previously safe jobs now face the threat of automation due to the development of artificial intelligence and automation. As a result, it's essential to keep learning new things to stay current and competitive in the employment market. By doing this, we raise our chances of landing well-paying jobs, getting promoted, and making more money, all of which can contribute to our ability to accumulate wealth.

Also, learning creates new possibilities for generating profit. For instance, a person who masters a new tongue can find employment as a translator or interpreter and make a respectable living doing so. A person who learns how to invest in the stock market can achieve a similarly high rate of return. As a result, by seeking out new knowledge, we improve our chances of discovering new business prospects.

Learning can aid us in developing new skills and knowledge as well as enhance our capacity for making decisions. We become more aware of the fundamental ideas and concepts of a subject as we learn more about it. As a result, we can make decisions more wisely and with more knowledge.

For instance, by learning the fundamentals of personal finance, we may make wiser choices regarding our debt management, savings, and investments, which can eventually help us build wealth.

Learning also aids in the development of critical thinking abilities, which are crucial for generating income. When we study a subject, we are exposed to various viewpoints, concepts, and arguments. This, therefore, aids in the development of our critical thinking abilities, allowing us to objectively assess material, recognize issues, and come up with solutions.
These critical thinking abilities are crucial for building wealth because they enable us to recognize new opportunities, assess risks, and make well-informed choices.

Finally, learning fosters the invention and creativity that are essential for generating wealth. When we study a certain topic, we are introduced to fresh notions, theories, and approaches. This in turn inspires our imagination and encourages creative problem-solving. For instance, by knowing about upcoming technology, we might generate fresh concepts for goods or services that can upend established markets and generate wealth.

In conclusion, education is a vital part of building wealth. We can improve our chances of making money by constantly learning new things, being relevant and competitive in the job market, and honing our critical thinking, creativity, and innovation skills.

To achieve financial success and stability, it is crucial to prioritize learning in both our personal and professional lives. Those that put learning first will be better positioned to take advantage of new opportunities and make money as the world continues to change quickly.

CHAPTER 6

FOUNDATIONS OF CREATING WEALTH

1.2. RISE TO RISK

It has long been understood that taking risks is an essential component of building wealth. Taking risks is frequently an essential step towards accumulating money, whether it's when starting a business, investing in the stock market, or making other financial decisions.

But, the idea of taking risks can be frightening and scary, which causes many people to completely avoid doing so. The importance of taking calculated risks for those who wish to succeed financially will be discussed in this essay along with how it plays a part in wealth development.

The ability to grow and expand is one of the most important ways that taking risks helps wealth creation. When people or companies take chances, they frequently have the opportunity to investigate uncharted markets or concepts.
They might be able to find fresh ways to make money and amass fortunes by doing this.

Also, by enabling them to adjust to shifting market conditions and stay ahead of the curve, taking risks can help people and businesses stay competitive.
It's important to remember, though, that taking risks does not always translate into success. In actuality, taking chances frequently entails the risk of failure or monetary loss. Some people's crippling dread of failure prevents them from taking any chances at all.

It's crucial to realize that failure does not always result in a bad conclusion. Failure can frequently be a fruitful learning experience that aids in the development and improvement of strategies for both people and businesses.

Furthermore, people who take chances and fail might be able to bounce back and perhaps experience even greater success in the long run.

The capacity to identify and manage risk efficiently is a crucial component of effective risk-taking. Those who can assess prospective risks and make wise decisions are more likely to succeed than others who take risks haphazardly without thorough thought.
This entails devoting time to research, comprehending the outcomes that could result from various options, and creating risk-reduction plans. A backup strategy

should also be in place in case things don't work out as planned.

Having the courage to act is another essential component of taking risks. Seeing the possible advantages of taking risks is one thing; taking the necessary action is quite another. Fear and uncertainty are common obstacles to taking action for many people. But those who can overcome these challenges and take prudent risks frequently achieve the greatest success in accumulating wealth.

It's also important to remember that taking risks is not just for business owners or entrepreneurs. Anybody can take chances to increase their wealth, whether it's through stock or real estate investing, a career change, or other means.

It's crucial to realize that different risks have varying degrees of potential profit and risk, though. For instance, stock investing carries a high amount of risk along with the potential for high profits. On the other hand, investing in real estate may provide more consistent profits but also require a sizable initial outlay.

The decision to take chances when building money is ultimately a personal one. While some people could feel at ease taking significant risks, others would choose to play it safe. It's crucial to realize, nevertheless, that taking chances is frequently a must for achieving financial success.

The most successful people at accumulating wealth are frequently those who can take calculated risks, do so successfully, and have the guts to act. Accepting risk-taking can help you reach your goals and create a more secure financial future, whether you're an entrepreneur, an investor, or simply someone wanting to improve their financial situation.

CHAPTER 7

FOUNDATIONS OF CREATING WEALTH

1.3. DISCIPLINE AND PERSISTENCE

Discipline and persistence are both necessary for building and sustaining wealth. These two traits are the primary fundamental building blocks for those who desire to realize their financial objectives and safeguard their future.

The capacity to adhere to a set of guidelines or a certain path of action is known as discipline. It involves having the self-control to adhere to a financial plan in any situation. This includes making a budget, establishing clear goals, and refraining from making rash purchases.

Another aspect of discipline is resisting the urge to overspend, take on debt that is beyond one's means, or make rash investments without doing sufficient research. Many people find it difficult to maintain financial discipline. Although they may have the best of intentions, they lack the discipline to carry out their strategy.

They might give in to the seduction of a new car, a lavish vacation, or the newest technological advancement. Even while they could be fun in the short run, these activities might be detrimental to one's long-term financial objectives.

Understanding one's financial objectives is crucial for developing discipline.
What do you hope to accomplish? Do you wish to clear your debt, put money down for a down payment on a home, or make

retirement investments? You may make a budget that supports your goals once you've decided what they are. All of your expenses, such as those for bills, groceries, entertainment, and savings, should be included in this budget.

You must monitor your expenditures if you want to stay within your budget. This entails keeping a list of every purchase you make and checking it frequently to make sure you are still on track. If your circumstances change over time, you might need to adapt your budget, but the most important thing is to keep your eyes on the prize.

For the production and preservation of wealth, persistence is just as important as discipline.
The trait of persistence is the ability to continue working toward a goal in the face of obstacles or disappointments. This refers to sticking with one's financial strategy even when the market is down or the results are

less than anticipated in the context of finance.
It also entails exercising patience and investing for the long term, resisting the urge to switch up your investments frequently to reap fast rewards.

Being persistent is crucial since wealth-building takes time. It necessitates constancy and dedication to the procedure. Along the journey, there will undoubtedly be obstacles and disappointments, but it is crucial to persevere and keep working toward your objectives.

This calls for a change of perspective from short-term to long-term thinking. Keep your eyes on the prize and strive toward your long-term goals rather than concentrating on short victories or instant gratification.
A plan must be in place to develop perseverance. This strategy should contain

explicit objectives, deadlines, and methods for accomplishing those objectives. A support system that can offer direction and accountability, such as a financial advisor or mentor, should be in place.

In conclusion, discipline and perseverance are crucial traits for building and maintaining money. Setting specific goals, making a budget, and abstaining from impulsive purchases are all necessary for developing discipline.

A long-term strategy, perseverance through difficulties, and staying the course are necessary for developing persistence. These traits work well together to provide a potent mix that can aid people in reaching their financial objectives and securing their future.
People may create and maintain a strong financial foundation that will allow them to experience financial security and freedom in

the long run by practicing discipline and perseverance.

CHAPTER 8

OVERCOMING OBSTACLES

It is difficult to become wealthy, and there are numerous challenges that one must overcome. These barriers may be internal such as fear, self-doubt, or a lack of motivation, or external such as a scarcity of resources or market volatility. Whatever the challenge, it's critical to have a plan in place to get over it and continue moving in the direction of your objectives.

Fear is one of the biggest roadblocks to financial success. Fear can appear in many different forms, including the dread of success, fear of taking chances, and fear of the unknown. It's crucial to realize that fear is a normal component of the process and that it can be conquered with the appropriate attitude and strategy.

Concentrating on your objectives and the advantages of reaching them is one strategy to get over your fear. You can stay motivated and overcome any fear or self-doubt that may develop by keeping your end objective in mind. It's also critical to keep in mind that failure is not the end of the path. Instead, it's a chance for you to improve and learn from your errors so that you can bounce back stronger.

Self-doubt is another frequent barrier to obtaining money. Many people experience imposter syndrome or believe they are not competent enough to accomplish their objectives. It's crucial to keep in mind that everyone has uncertainties and that it's common to occasionally feel unsure. The important thing is to not let self-doubt stop you from following your goals.

Consider your accomplishments and strengths as a technique to combat self-doubt. Think back on your prior accomplishments and the talents and skills that have enabled you to succeed in achieving them. Moreover, surround yourself with positive individuals who have faith in your talents and can offer assistance when required.

A further typical barrier to earning wealth is a lack of resources. This might be due to a lack of resources, such as money, as well as a lack of time, resources, or relationships.
It's crucial to realize that resources are always accessible; it's up to you to find them and utilize them effectively.

Being resourceful is one way to get over a lack of resources. This entails coming up with original solutions and making use of the resources you already have. For instance, start small and gradually increase your investments over time if you don't have much money to invest. Instead, if you're short on time, look for ways to automate or streamline your accounts to free up more time for your wealth plan.

Another important aspect of conquering challenges and gaining money is remaining motivated. When faced with obstacles or disappointments, it's simple to lose motivation or focus. When things get difficult, it's crucial to maintain motivation and focus on your objectives.

Celebrate your small victories along the way as a strategy to keep motivated. This might include modest victories like sticking to your spending plan or saving your designated amount, as well as more substantial ones like launching a flourishing business or generating a sizeable investment return. Also, it's critical to never lose sight of the motivations for your pursuit of money.

When the going gets tough, this can keep you inspired and committed to your objectives.

In conclusion, gaining riches entails conquering both internal and external challenges. These difficulties may be brought on by fear, self-doubt, a shortage of supplies, or a lack of drive. Nonetheless, these challenges can be overcome with the appropriate perspective and strategy.

You can overcome any challenge and attain the financial stability and independence you want by being motivated, staying focused on your goals, and making the most of your resources.

CHAPTER 9

PRESERVING WEALTH

Although becoming wealthy is a significant accomplishment, it is only the beginning. Focus on preserving your wealth and creating a sustainable financial future once you have attained financial independence and stability.

This calls for thorough preparation, wise money management, and ongoing investment in your future and self. Effective money management is one of the key components of wealth preservation. This entails setting up and adhering to a budget, keeping tabs on your spending, and making smart financial decisions.

Building an emergency fund and having a good strategy in place for unforeseen costs or changes in your financial circumstances are also crucial.

Building a solid support network is a crucial aspect of retaining wealth.
This entails having a dependable accountant or financial counselor to assist you in making wise investing selections, as well as friends and family who can provide support and encouragement.

It's crucial to surround oneself with people who share your ideals and financial aspirations.
Maintaining wealth also depends on continuing to invest in oneself. To stay relevant and competitive in your work, you must invest in your education, skills, and professional growth.

It also entails taking good care of your physical and emotional well-being, which can have long-term effects on your financial security.

Setting aside time and money for personal development is one way to invest in oneself. This can entail enrolling in seminars or workshops to pick up new skills, going to conferences or networking events to meet people in the business world, or hiring a coach or mentor to offer direction and assistance.
Setting your health and well-being as a priority is another way to invest in yourself. This can entail setting aside time each day for exercise, eating a balanced diet, and relaxing.

To make wise financial decisions and keep your money over the long term, it's also critical to manage stress and prevent burnout.

It's crucial to keep up with changes in the financial scene in addition to managing your funds, developing a solid support network, and investing in yourself.
This entails staying current with market developments, tax regulations, and economic factors that may affect your financial planning and investments.

In general, wealth maintenance calls for initiative and a dedication to continual development. You can make sure that your wealth endures over the long term by managing your money wisely, creating a strong support network, investing in yourself, and keeping up with changes in the financial landscape.

CHAPTER 10

INVESTMENT AS A MEANS OF PRESERVING WEALTH

Everyone aspires to acquire wealth at some point in their lives since it is a desirable item. It serves as a gauge of one's financial situation and capacity to pay for needs and wants.

But acquiring wealth alone is insufficient; preserving it is just as crucial. If wealth is not properly managed, it can be lost just as quickly as it is earned. When it comes to preserving wealth, investments can help.

The act of investing involves placing money into a business or asset with the hope of making a profit. Making a return on one's investment is the aim of investing, which could take the form of dividends, interest, or capital gains.

There are many different types of investment opportunities, including stocks, bonds, real estate, and mutual funds. In order to maintain their wealth, people invest for a variety of reasons. By increasing their assets and creating a continuous stream of income, investors help people maintain their wealth.

For long-term financial security, especially in the face of inflation and market instability, wealth preservation is essential. Inflation is the term used to describe the gradual upward trend in product and service prices over time. Money loses value and has less purchasing power as a result. Investments must be made in assets that can outpace inflation as a result.

Stocks and real estate are examples of investments that have the potential to increase in value over time and can act as a hedge against inflation. These assets can aid investors in preserving the purchasing power of their wealth as their value increases.

Another element that may affect a person's wealth is market volatility. For instance, the stock market may see abrupt and significant changes in value as a result of a variety of variables, including the state of the economy, current political events, and company performance.

The risk of market volatility can be reduced by investing in a diverse portfolio of assets. Investing in a variety of assets across various industries and regions constitutes diversification. This strategy can assist in distributing risk and lessen the effect of market changes on a person's overall wealth.

Investments offer a way to make money as well. Certain investments, such as bonds and stocks, in the form of dividends and interest payments, offer consistent income. This revenue can be utilized to pay for living needs or reinvested to increase one's wealth. For instance, retirees can increase their retirement income by purchasing dividend-paying equities or bonds.

Moreover, an investment may be a way to meet long-term financial objectives. People can build wealth and reach financial milestones like purchasing a home, covering their children's college expenses, or retiring comfortably by investing in assets that have the potential to increase in value over time.

A financial legacy for future generations can be left through investing.

The dangers associated with investing must be understood by investors, though. Investment value is subject to change. Investors could not get their entire investment back if the market goes up as well as down.

In addition, some investments, like stocks and real estate, can be unstable and vulnerable to sharp value changes. So, investors must adopt a responsible and knowledgeable investing strategy. Before purchasing any asset, they should conduct due diligence and seek the counsel of financial professionals. Having a long-term investment horizon and understanding the risks and potential benefits of any investment opportunity is essential.

Finally, investing is a way to keep your wealth. Increasing their assets and producing a consistent flow of income, enables people to maintain the value of their money over time. Investments can provide long-term financial security by insulating against the depleting impacts of inflation and market volatility.

Yet, there are risks associated with investing, and investors need to be aware of these risks. To preserve and increase one's money over the long run, investing should be done carefully and with knowledge.

CHAPTER 11

LEADING A PROSPEROUS LIFE

While acquiring material riches is undoubtedly a good objective, it's crucial to understand that true wealth entails much more than just money.
Leading a prosperous life entails seeking happiness and meaning in all areas of your life and leading a fulfilling existence.

Having a rewarding career is essential to having a prosperous life. This entails finding work that is in line with your interests and values and that enables you to have a significant impact on the world.

Prioritizing work-life balance and finding a career that enables you to maintain a healthy and sustainable lifestyle is equally crucial.

Maintaining meaningful relationships is a crucial component of living a prosperous life. This entails spending time and effort cultivating close relationships with friends, family, and other loved ones. It also entails encouraging a sense of community and belonging and meaningfully helping others.

Having a wealthy life also entails pursuing your interests and finding happiness and fulfillment in the activities you enjoy. This could be developing a creative outlet, participating in outdoor pursuits, or giving your time to a cause you care about. You can develop a sense of purpose and meaning in your life by pursuing the things that make you happy and following your passions.

Another essential component of leading a wealthy life is giving back to your community and having a positive impact on the globe. This entails figuring out how to use your abilities, assets, and free time to assist others and change the world. This could entail giving your time to a neighborhood nonprofit or charity, making a donation to an important cause, or using your expertise to mentor and help others.

Finding harmony and fulfillment in all areas of your life is ultimately the key to having a wealthy life. It's about realizing that pleasure and significance come from a combination of a career, relationships, passions, and purpose, and that true riches cover much more than just financial wealth.

By emphasizing these facets of your life, as well as by developing a spirit of thankfulness and gratitude you may build a life of prosperity and fulfillment that goes beyond material wealth by being generous.

CONCLUSION

In conclusion, wealth is a mindset that entails fostering an attitude of abundance and thankfulness in all spheres of your life, rather than just the quantity of money in your bank account.

You may position yourself for success and build a life of fulfillment and meaning by developing a wealthy mindset. Setting goals, making a budget, investing in oneself, taking cautious chances, overcoming challenges, maintaining riches, and leading a life that extends beyond merely material prosperity are all necessary to achieve this.

You may unlock your potential by realizing that true riches are about more than simply money and by developing an attitude of abundance.
Reach your best potential and succeed in all spheres of your life.